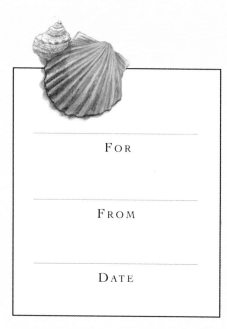

For

From

Date

Poems to Comfort

THOUGHTS TO ENCOURAGE

ART BY
GLENDA PUHEK

IDEALS PUBLICATIONS, A DIVISION OF GUIDEPOSTS
NASHVILLE, TENNESSEE

ISBN 0-8249-4123-3

Caseside printed in the U.S.A.
Text printed and bound in Mexico.
Printed by R.R. Donnelley & Sons.

Published by Ideals Publications, a division of Guideposts
535 Metroplex Drive, Suite 250
Nashville, Tennessee 37211
www.idealspublications.com

Library of Congress Cataloging-in-Publication Data

Poems to comfort: thoughts to encourage / art by Glenda Puhek.
    p. cm.
    Includes index.
    ISBN 0-8249-4123-3 (alk. paper)
    1. Religious poetry, American. 2. Encouragement--Poetry. I. Puhek, Glenda.

PS595.R4 P64 2001
811.008'0382--dc21   2001024655

10 8 6 4 2 1 3 5 7 9

POEMS SELECTED BY PATRICIA A. PINGRY
DESIGNED BY EVE DEGRIE

ACKNOWLEDGMENTS

CROWELL, GRACE NOLL. "Hope" from *Poems of Inspiration and Courage*. Copyright © 1928, 1934 by Harper & Row Publishers, Inc.
Renewed 1956, 1962 by Grace Noll Crowell. Used by permission of HarperCollins Publishers, Inc. JACOBS, MILDRED SPIRES.
"Peace." Used by permission of the author. KLEMME, MINNIE. "Hope for Tomorrow." Used by permission of the author. SANTAYANA,
GEORGE. "O World" from *Poems*. Copyright © 1933 by Charles Scribner's Sons. Used by permission of MIT Press. SPRINGSTEEN,
ANNE. "This Morning." Used by permission of the author's estate. STIDGER, WILLIAM L. "A Day." Used by permission of the author's
estate. STRONG, PATIENCE. "The Unbroken String." Used by permission of Rupert Crew Limited. Our sincere thanks to the follow-
ing authors whom we were unable to locate: Julia A. Baker for "Mizpah"; Thomas Curtis Clark for "The Search"; Ralph Spaulding
Cushman for "I Will Not Hurry"; Annie Johnson Flint for "What God Hath Promised"; Spencer Michael Free for "The Human
Touch"; Florence Scripps Kellogg for "My Hand in God's"; Bernice C. Plautz for "My Guide"; A. W. Spalding for "High Adventure."

CONTENTS

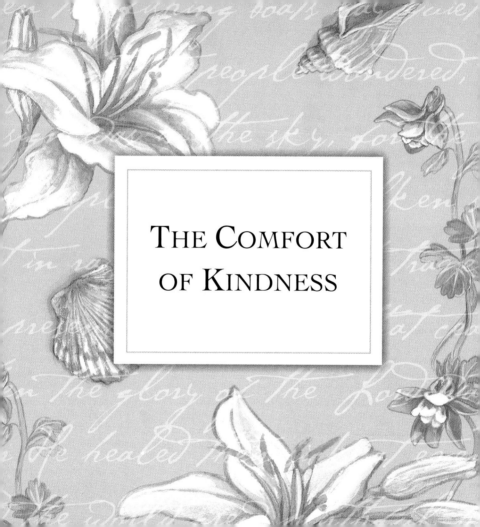

THE COMFORT
OF KINDNESS

Comfort

Oh, the comfort—
The inexpressible comfort
Of feeling safe with a person,
Having neither to weigh thoughts,
Nor measure words—
But pouring them
All right out—
Just as they are—
Chaff and grain together—
Certain that a faithful hand
Will take and sift them—
Keep what is worth keeping—
And with the breath of kindness
Blow the rest away.

—Dinah Maria Mulock Craik

ABOU BEN ADHEM

Abou Ben Adhem (may his tribe increase!)
Awoke one night from a deep dream of peace,
And saw, within the moonlight in his room,
Making it rich, and like a lily in bloom,
An Angel writing in a book of gold:
Exceeding peace had made Ben Adhem bold,
And to the Presence in the room he said,
"What writest thou?" The Vision raised its head,
And with a look made of all sweet accord
Answered, "The names of those who love the Lord."

"And is mine one?" said Abou. "Nay, not so,"
Replied the Angel. Abou spoke more low,
But cheerily still; and said, "I pray thee, then,
Write me as one that loves his fellow men."

The Angel wrote, and vanished. The next night
It came again with a great wakening light,
And showed the names whom love of God had blessed,
And, lo! Ben Adhem's name led all the rest!
—JAMES HENRY LEIGH HUNT

MIZPAH

Go thou thy way, and I go mine,
Apart, yet not afar;
Only a thin veil hangs between
The pathways where we are.
And "God keep watch 'tween thee and me";
This is my prayer;
He looks thy way, He looketh mine,
    And keeps us near.

I know not where thy road may lie,
Or which way mine will be;
If mine will lead thro' parching sands
And thine beside the sea;
Yet God keeps watch 'tween thee and me,
So never fear.
He holds thy hands, He claspeth mine,
And keeps us near.

I sigh sometimes to see thy face,
But since this may not be,
I'll leave thee to the care of Him
Who cares for thee and me.
"I'll keep you both beneath my wings,"
This comforts, dear;
One wing o'er thee and one o'er me,
Will keep us near.

And though our paths be separate,
And thy way is not mine,
Yet coming to the Mercy seat,
My soul will meet with thine.
And "God keep watch 'tween thee and me,"
I'll whisper there.
He blesseth thee, He blesseth me,
And we are near.

—JULIA A. BAKER

WISDOM

For this is wisdom;
To love, to live,
To take what fate,
Or the gods, may give,
To ask no question,
To make no prayer,
To kiss the lips
And caress the hair,
Speed passion's ebb
As you greet its flow, —
To have, to hold,
And, in time, let go.
— LAURENCE HOPE

THE COMFORT OF KINDNESS

A Day

What does it take to make a day?
A lot of love along the way:
It takes a morning and a noon,
A father's voice, a mother's croon;
It takes some task to challenge all
The powers that a man may call
His own: the powers of mind and limb;
A whispered word of love; a hymn
Of hope — a comrade's cheer —
A baby's laughter and a tear;

It takes a dream, a hope, a cry
Of need from some soul passing by;
A sense of brotherhood and love;
A purpose sent from God above;
It takes a sunset in the sky,
The stars of night, the winds that sigh;
It takes a breath of scented air,
A mother's kiss, a baby's prayer.
That is what it takes to make a day;
A lot of love along the way.

—WILLIAM L. STIDGER

KINDNESS

Do all the good you can,
By all the means you can,
In all the ways you can,
In all the places you can,
At all the times you can,
To all the people you can,
As long as ever you can.

— JOHN WESLEY

REWARD OF SERVICE

The sweetest lives are those to duty wed,
Whose deeds, both great and small,
Are close-knit strands of an unbroken thread
Where love ennobles all.
The world may sound no trumpets, ring no bells,
The Book of Life the slurring record tells.

Thy love shall chant its own beatitudes
After its own like working. A child's kiss
Set on thy singing lips shall make thee rich;
A sick man helped by thee shall make thee strong;
Thou shalt be served thyself by every sense
Of service which thou renderest.

— ELIZABETH BARRETT BROWNING

POEMS TO COMFORT

THE HUMAN TOUCH

'Tis the human touch in this world that counts,
The touch of your hand and mine,
Which means far more to the fainting heart
Than shelter and bread and wine;

For shelter is gone when the night is o'er,
And bread lasts only a day,
But the touch of the hand
   and the sound of the voice
Sing on in the soul alway.
— SPENCER MICHAEL FREE

How He Came

When the golden evening gathered on the shore of Galilee,
When the fishing boats lay quiet by the sea,
Long ago the people wondered, tho' no sign was in the sky,
For the glory of the Lord was passing by.

Not in robes of purple splendor, not in silken softness shod,
But in raiment worn with travel came their God,
And the people knew His presence by the heart that ceased to sigh
When the glory of the Lord was passing by.

For He healed their sick at even, and He cured the leper's sore,
And sinful men and women sinned no more,
And the world grew mirthful-hearted, and forgot its misery
When the glory of the Lord was passing by.

Not in robes of purple splendor, but in lives that do His will,
In patient acts of kindness He comes still;
And the people cry with wonder, tho' no sign is in the sky,
That the glory of the Lord is passing by.
— W. J. DAWSON

My Beloved Ones

Lord, make me one with Thine own faithful ones,
Thy saints who love Thee and are loved by Thee;
Till the day break and till the shadows flee
At one with them in alms and orisons:
At one with him who toils and him who runs,
And him who yearns for union yet to be;
   At one with all who throng the crystal sea
   And wait the setting of our moons and suns.

   Ah, my beloved ones gone on before,
   Who looked not back with hand upon the plough!
If beautiful to me while still in sight,
How beautiful must be your aspects now;
Your unknown, well-known aspects in that light
Which clouds shall never cloud forevermore.

—Christina Georgina Rossetti

I Shall Not Live in Vain

If I can stop one heart from breaking
I shall not live in vain;
If I can ease one life the aching,
Or cool one pain,
Or help one fainting robin
Unto his nest again,
I shall not live in vain.

— EMILY DICKINSON

At Even, When the Sun Was Set

At even, when the sun was set,
The sick, O Lord, around Thee lay;
O in what divers pains they met;
  O with what joy they went away.

Once more 'tis eventide, and we,
Oppressed with various ills, draw near;
What if Thy form we cannot see,
We know and feel that Thou art here.

O Saviour Christ, our woes dispel;
For some are sick, and some are sad,
And some have never loved Thee well,
And some have lost the love they had;

And some are pressed with worldly care,
And some are tried with sinful doubt;

And some such grievous passions tear,
That only Thou canst cast them out;

And some have found the world is vain,
Yet from the world they break not free;
And some have friends who give them pain,
Yet have not sought a Friend in Thee;

And none, O Lord, have perfect rest,
For none are wholly free from sin;
And they who fain would serve Thee best
Are conscious most of wrong within.

Thy touch has still its ancient power;
No word from Thee can fruitless fall;
Hear, in this solemn evening hour,
And in Thy mercy heal us all.

—HENRY TWELLS

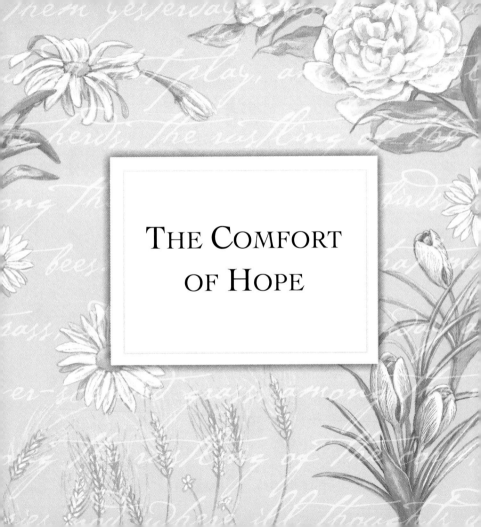

THE COMFORT
OF HOPE

Look to This Day

Look to this day! For it is life,
The very life of life.
In its brief course lie all the verities
And realities of your existence:

The bliss of growth; the glory of action;
The splendor of beauty;
For yesterday is already a dream,
And tomorrow is only a vision;

But today, well lived,
Makes every yesterday a dream of happiness,
And every tomorrow a vision of hope.
Look well, therefore, to this day!

—FROM THE SANSKRIT

Two Carefree Days

There are two days in the week about
Which and upon which I never worry.
Two carefree days, kept sacredly free
From fear and apprehension.
    One of these days is Yesterday.

Yesterday with all its cares and frets,
With all its pains and aches,
All its faults, and its mistakes and blunders,
Has passed forever beyond the reach of my recall.
I cannot undo an act that I wrought.
I cannot unsay a word that I said
    On Yesterday.

All that it holds of my life,
Of wrong, regret, and sorrow
Is in the hands of the Mighty Love
That can bring honey out of the rock
And sweet waters out of the bitterest desert.
And the other day I do not worry about is Tomorrow.
Tomorrow with all its possible adversities, its burdens,
Its perils, its large promise and poor performance,
Its failures and mistakes, is as far beyond the reach of my mastery
    As its dead sister, Yesterday.
— ROBERT J. BURDETTE

GOD

There is an Eye that never sleeps
Beneath the wing of night;
There is an ear that never shuts
When sink the beams of light.

There is an arm that never tires
When human strength gives way;
There is a love that never fails
When earthly loves decay.

That Eye unseen o'erwatcheth all;
That Arm upholds the sky;
That Ear doth hear the sparrows call;
That Love is ever nigh.

— JAMES COWDEN WALLACE

I NEVER KNEW A NIGHT SO BLACK

I never knew a night so black
Light failed to follow on its track.
I never knew a storm so gray
It failed to have its clearing day.
I never knew such bleak despair
That there was not a rift, somewhere.
I never knew an hour so drear
Love could not fill it full of cheer!

—JOHN KENDRICK BANGS

The Unbroken String

Love and friendship, joy and sorrow,
These are the strings on which we play.
These are the notes that go to make
The varied music of the day.

With the passing of the years
The strings of life get frayed and thin—

And youth's high tones are touched
With sadness, like a muted violin.

But there is one undying thing,
One golden string that does not break:
The string of Hope —
We play upon it, and it never fails to wake
An echo in the weary spirit.
One sweet note fresh faith can bring.

For Hope is the music of the soul
Played on the heart's unbroken string.
— PATIENCE STRONG

I WILL NOT HURRY

I will not hurry through this day!
Lord, I will listen by the way,
To humming bees and singing birds,
To speaking trees and friendly words;
And, for the moments in between,
Seek glimpses of Thy great Unseen.

I will not hurry through this day;
I will take time to think and pray;
I will look up into the sky,
Where fleecy clouds and swallows fly;
And, somewhere in the day, maybe
I will catch whispers, Lord, from Thee!
— RALPH SPAULDING CUSHMAN

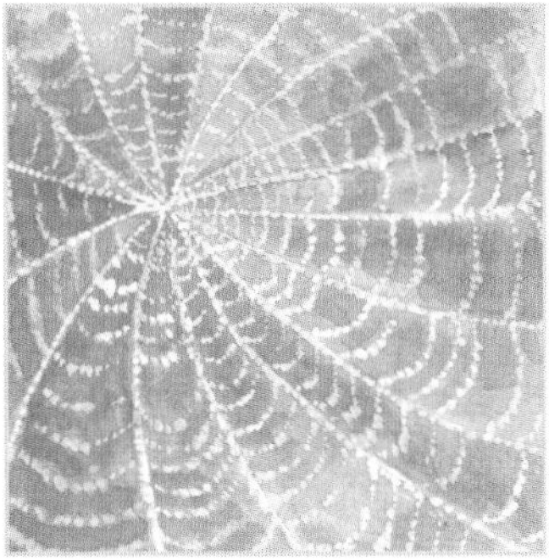

HOPE

This would I hold more precious than fine gold,
This would I keep although all else be lost:
Hope in my heart, that precious, priceless thing,
    hope at any cost.

And God, if its fine luster should be dimmed,
If seemingly through grief it may be spent,
    Help me to wait without too much despair —
        too great astonishment.

Let me be patient when my spirit lacks
Its high exuberance, its shining wealth;
Hope is a matter often, God, I know,
　　of strength . . . of health.

Help me to wait until the strength returns;
Help me to climb each difficult high slope;
Always within my heart some golden gleam—
　　some quenchless spark of hope.

　—GRACE NOLL CROWELL

Out in the Fields with God

The little cares that fretted me,
I lost them yesterday
Among the fields above the sea,
Among the winds that play,
Among the lowing of the herds,
The rustling of the trees,
Among the singing of the birds,
The humming of the bees.

The fears of what may come to pass,
I cast them all away
Among the clover-scented grass,
Among the new-mown hay,
Among the rustling of the corn,
Where drowsy poppies nod,
Where ill thoughts die and good are born,
Out in the fields with God.

—AUTHOR UNKNOWN

POEMS TO COMFORT

HOPE FOR TOMORROW

Hope thinks tomorrow will be brighter;
Faith knows,
And, knowing, is the surer of the two,
And makes it true.

But when the morrow lengthens into night
And shadows throng,
Hope, like another dawn, transfuses faith
And makes it strong.

— MINNIE KLEMME

WHAT GOD HATH PROMISED

God hath not promised
Skies always blue,
Flower-strewn pathways
All our lives through;
God hath not promised
Sun without rain,
Joy without sorrow,
Peace without pain.

But God hath promised
Strength for the day,
Rest for the labor,
Light for the way,
Grace for the trials,
Help from above,
Unfailing sympathy,
Undying love.

—ANNIE JOHNSON FLINT

A Psalm of Life

Tell me not, in mournful numbers,
Life is but an empty dream! —
For the soul is dead that slumbers,
And things are not what they seem.

Life is real! Life is earnest!
And the grave is not its goal;
Dust thou art, to dust returnest,
Was not spoken of the soul.

Not enjoyment, and not sorrow
Is our destined end or way;
But to act, that each tomorrow
Find us farther than today.

Lives of great men all remind us
We can make our lives sublime,
And, departing, leave behind us
Footprints on the sand of time —

Footprints, that perhaps another,
Sailing o'er life's solemn main,
A forlorn and shipwrecked brother,
Seeing, shall take heart again.

Let us, then, be up and doing,
With a heart for any fate;
Still achieving, still pursuing,
Learn to labor and to wait.

— HENRY WADSWORTH LONGFELLOW

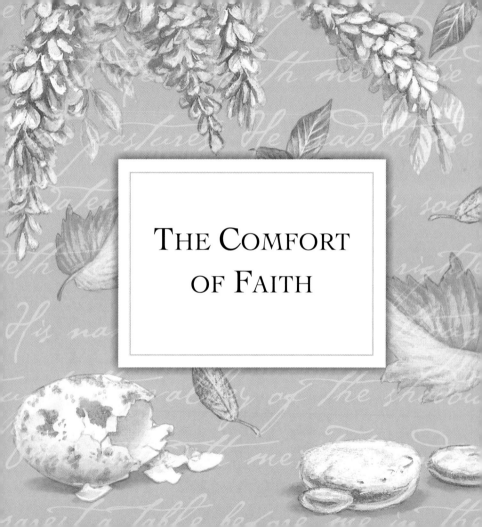

THE COMFORT
OF FAITH

THIS MORNING

Life has begun again, Father.
You have given me another day of grace,
Another day to live;
    to speak to someone,
    to touch someone,
    to ask for something,
    to take something,
    to give something.

Whatever I make of this day,
Whatever I become this day
I put into Your hands.
— ANNE SPRINGSTEEN

I HAVE SEEN A CURIOUS CHILD

I have seen
A curious child, who dwelt upon a tract
Of inland ground, applying to his ear
The convolutions of a smooth-lipped shell;
To which, in silence hushed, his very soul
Listened intensely; and his countenance soon
Brightened with joy; for from within were heard
Murmurings, whereby the monitor expressed
Mysterious union with its native sea.
Even such a shell the universe itself
Is to the ear of Faith; and there are times,

I doubt not, when to you it doth impart
Authentic tidings of invisible things;
Of ebb and flow, and ever-during power;
And central peace, subsisting at the heart
Of endless agitation.
— WILLIAM WORDSWORTH

"ARE YOU THERE?"

I like to play close by my father's den,
    Where he's at work, and every now and then
Ask, "Father, are you there?" He answers back,
"Yes, son." That time I broke my railroad track
All into bits, he stopped his work and came
And wiped my tears, and said, "Boy, boy! Be game!"
And then he showed me how to fix it right,
And I took both my arms and hugged him tight.

Once, when I'd asked him if he still was there,
He called me in and rumpled up my hair,
And said, "How much alike are you and I!
When I feel just as boys feel when they cry,
I call to our Big Father, to make sure
That He is there, my childish dread to cure.
And always, just as I to you, 'Yes, son,'
Our Father calls, and all my fret is done!"
— STRICKLAND GILLILAN

The Lord Is My Shepherd

The Lord is my shepherd; I shall not want.
He maketh me to lie down in green pastures:
He leadeth me beside the still waters. He restoreth my soul:
He leadeth me in the paths of righteousness for His name's sake.
Yea, though I walk through the valley of the shadow of death,
I will fear no evil: for Thou art with me;
Thy rod and Thy staff they comfort me.
Thou preparest a table before me in the presence of mine enemies:
Thou anointest my head with oil; my cup runneth over.

Surely goodness and mercy shall follow me all the days of my life:
And I will dwell in the house of the Lord for ever.

—Psalm 23

THE COMFORT OF FAITH 53

NATURE

As a fond mother, when the day is o'er,
Leads by the hand her little child to bed,
Half willing, half reluctant to be led,
And leaves his broken playthings on the floor,
Still gazing at them through the open door,
Nor wholly reassured and comforted
By promises of others in their stead,
Which, though more splendid, may not please him more:

So Nature deals with us, and takes away
Our playthings one by one, and by the hand
Leads us to rest so gently, that we go
Scarce knowing if we wish to go or stay,
Being too full of sleep to understand
How far the unknown transcends what we know.

— HENRY WADSWORTH LONGFELLOW

HE HEARS WITH GLADDENED HEART

He hears with gladdened heart the thunder
Peal, and loves the falling dew;
He knows the earth above and under—
Sits and is content to view.

He sits beside the dying ember,
God for hope and man for friend,
Content to see, glad to remember,
Expectant of the certain end.

—ROBERT LOUIS STEVENSON

HIGH ADVENTURE

As I have seen a child,
Round-eyed and innocent,
Leaving his treasured playthings piled
Where new adventure overtook,
Climb up a little staired ascent,
Holding in fear his parent's hand,
And, trepidant with fresh alarms
Yet gathering courage from each trustful look,
With utter confidence in a last command,
Fling himself laughing into his father's arms—

So I, another child,
 Holding my Father's hand,
   Now from my busy arts beguiled
   By what He promises beyond,
Forgetting all that I have planned,
And pressing on with faith's sure sight
O'er rock and ridge, through mists and storms,
With confidence that swallows up despond,
From the last crag of life's most glorious height
Cast me exultant into my Father's arms.
—A. W. Spalding

POEMS TO COMFORT

O WORLD

O world, thou choosest not the better part!
It is not wisdom to be only wise,
And on the inward vision close the eyes,
But it is wisdom to believe the heart.
Columbus found a world and had no chart
Save one that faith deciphered in the skies;
To trust the soul's invincible surmise
Was all his science and his only art.
Our knowledge is a torch of smoky pine
That lights the pathway but one step ahead
Across a void of mystery and dread.
Bid then the tender light of faith to shine
By which alone the mortal heart is led
Unto the thinking of the thought divine.

— GEORGE SANTAYANA

My Hand in God's

Each morning when I wake I say,
"I place my hand in God's today."
I know He'll walk close by my side,
My every wandering step to guide.

He leads me with the tenderest care
When paths are dark and I despair.
No need for me to understand,
If I but hold fast to His hand.

My hand in His! No surer way
To walk in safety through each day.
By His great bounty I am fed,
Warmed by His love and comforted.

When at day's end I seek my rest
And realize how much I'm blessed,
My thanks pour out to Him; and then
I place my hand in God's again.
—FLORENCE SCRIPPS KELLOGG

EVENSONG

The embers of the day are red
Beyond the murky hill.
The kitchen smokes;
The bed in the darkling
House is spread:
The great sky darkens overhead,
And the great woods are shrill.
So far have I been led,
Lord, by Thy will:
So far have I followed,
Lord, and wondered still.

The breeze from the
Embalmed land
Blows sudden towards the shore,
And claps my cottage door.
I hear the signal, Lord—
I understand.
The night at Thy command
Comes.
I will eat and sleep and
Will not question more.
—ROBERT LOUIS STEVENSON

My Guide

"Walk close to Me, my child," he said,
And on the way, He gently led;
"I know the way, it's very steep,
But do not fear, for I can keep
Your way secure; just trust Me more."
And so I walk the road of life —
My hand in His; no fear, no strife;
He keeps my heart rejoicing
In every testing; none is too great.
Because of Him my heart is singing;
He leads the way through every day.
I'm in this world for just a while;
I'll trust Him when I go through trials.
And often as I kneel and pray
I ask Him for the words to say
So others will be drawn to Him

By what they see of Him in me.
I ask Him to show me the need
Of each one for whom I should pray,
The ones I meet from day to day.
He guides my thoughts, my lips, my feet,
And teaches me just how to speak—
Sometimes, with joy, sometimes a warning,
Always with love to meet their longing.
I never fear with Him to guide,
On the stony road I do not fall;
I have my Friend close by my side;
I cling to Him when I feel weak;
He always hears me when I call.
He never fails! His strength is mine;
I walk with Him in joy sublime!

—BERNICE C. PLAUTZ

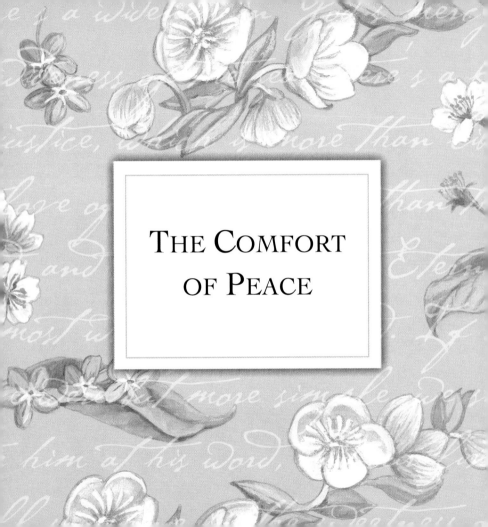

THE COMFORT
OF PEACE

One Day at a Time

Finish every day and be done with it.
You have done what you could.
Some blunders and absurdities no doubt crept in;
Forget them as soon as you can.

Tomorrow is a new day;
Begin it well and serenely
And with too high a spirit to be cumbered
With your old nonsense.

This day is all that is good and fair.
It is too dear,
With its hopes and invitations,
To waste a moment on the yesterdays.

— Ralph Waldo Emerson

THE DAY IS DONE

The day is done, and the darkness
Falls from the wings of Night,
As a feather is wafted downward
From an eagle in his flight.

Come, read to me some poem,
Some simple and heartfelt lay,
That shall soothe this restless feeling,
And banish the thoughts of day.

Read from some humbler poet,
Whose songs gush'd from his heart,
As showers from the clouds of summer,
Or tears from the eyelids start;

Who, through long days of labor,
And nights devoid of ease,

Still heard in his soul the music
Of wonderful melodies.

Such songs have power to quiet
The restless pulse of care,
And come like the benediction
That follows after prayer.

Then read from the treasured volume
The poem of thy choice;
And lend to the rhyme of the poet
The beauty of thy voice.

And the night shall be fill'd with music,
And the cares that infest the day
Shall fold their tents like the Arabs,
And as silently steal away.

— HENRY WADSWORTH LONGFELLOW

Up-Hill

Does the road wind up-hill all the way?
  Yes, to the very end.
Will the day's journey take the whole long day?
  From morn to night, my friend.

But is there for the night a resting-place?
  A roof for when the slow dark hours begin.
May not the darkness hide it from my face?
  You cannot miss that inn.

Shall I meet other wayfarers at night?
  Those who have gone before.

Then must I knock, or call when just in sight?
They will not keep you standing at that door.

Shall I find comfort, travel-sore and weak?
Of labour you shall find the sum.
Will there be beds for me and all who seek?
Yea, beds for all who come.

—CHRISTINA GEORGINA ROSSETTI

THE COMFORT OF PEACE

71

PEACE

Peace is looking at a child
With eyelids closed in sleep
And knowing that the love of God
Is constant, true and deep.

Peace is gazing into depths
Of water, cool and clear,
And knowing fast within your heart
That God is ever near.

Peace is living day by day
With His own company,
So you will have within your soul
Divine tranquility.

—MILDRED SPIRES JACOBS

ALL THROUGH THE NIGHT

Sleep, my love, and peace attend thee,
All through the night;
Guardian angels God will lend thee,
All through the night;
Soft the drowsy hours are creeping,
Hill and dale in slumber steeping,
Love alone his watch is keeping—
All through the night.

Hark! a solemn bell is ringing,
Clear through the night;
Thou, my love, art heavenward winging,
Home through the night;
Earthly dust from off thee shaken,
Soul immortal thou shalt waken,
With thy last dim journey taken
Home through the night.

—AUTHOR UNKNOWN

CROSSING THE BAR

Sunset and evening star,
And one clear call for me!
And may there be no moaning of the bar,
When I put out to sea,

But such a tide as moving seems asleep,
Too full for sound and foam,
When that which drew from out
    the boundless deep
Turns again home.

Twilight and evening bell,
And after that the dark!
And may there be no sadness of farewell,
When I embark;

For tho' from out our bourne of Time and Place
The flood may bear me far,
I hope to see my Pilot face to face
When I have crossed the bar.

— ALFRED, LORD TENNYSON

POEMS TO COMFORT

THE SEARCH

I sought His love in sun and stars,
And where the wild seas roll,
And found it not. As mute I stood,
Fear overwhelmed my soul;
But when I gave to one in need,
I found the Lord of Love indeed.

I sought His love in lore of books,
In charts of science' skill;
They left me orphaned as before—
His love eluded still;
Then in despair I breathed a prayer;
The Lord of Love was standing there!

—THOMAS CURTIS CLARK

A CHILD'S THOUGHT OF GOD

They say that God lives very high!
But if you look above the pines
You cannot see our God. And why?

And if you dig down in the mines
You never see Him in the gold;
Though from Him all that's glory shines.

God is so good, He wears a fold
Of heaven and earth across His face —
Like secrets kept, for love untold.

But still I feel that His embrace
Slides down by thrills, through all things made,
Through sight and sound of every place:

As if my tender mother laid
On my shut lids her kisses' pressure,
Half-waking me at night, and said,
"Who kissed you through the dark, dear guesser?"
—ELIZABETH BARRETT BROWNING

The Heart of the Eternal

There's a wideness in God's mercy,
Like the wideness of the sea;
There's a kindness in His justice,
Which is more than liberty.

For the love of God is broader
Than the measures of man's mind;
And the heart of the Eternal
Is most wonderfully kind.

If our love were but more simple,
We should take Him at His word,
And our lives would be all sunshine
In the sweetness of our Lord.

—FREDERICK W. FABER

O MASTER, LET ME WALK WITH THEE

O Master, let me walk with Thee
In lowly paths of service free;
Tell me Thy secret; help me bear
The strain of toil, the fret of care.

Help me the slow of heart to move
By some clear, winning word of love;
Teach me the wayward feet to stay
And guide them in the homeward way.

In hope that sends a shining ray
Far down the future's broadening way;
In peace that only Thou canst give, —
With Thee, O Master, let me live!

— WASHINGTON GLADDEN

High Flight

Oh! I have slipped the surly bonds of Earth
And danced the skies on laughter-silvered wings;
Sunward I've climbed, and joined the tumbling mirth
Of sun-split clouds—and done a hundred things
You have not dreamed of—wheeled and soared and swung
High in the sunlit silence. Hov'ring there,
I've chased the shouting wind along, and flung
My eager craft through footless halls of air. . . .

Up, up the long, delirious, burning blue
I've topped the wind-swept heights with easy grace,
Where never lark, or even eagle, flew;
And, while with silent, lifting mind I've trod
The high untrespassed sanctity of space,
Put out my hand, and touched the face of God.

— JOHN GILLESPIE MAGEE JR.

TITLE INDEX

First Line Index

FIRST LINE INDEX

Author Index